I0116800

INNOCENT

WISDOM

BY NATHAN HAMMAH

A NATHAN HAMMAH NOVEL PUBLISHED BY

WTL INTERNATIONAL

INNOCENT WISDOM

Published by
WTL International
930 North Park Drive
P.O. Box 33049
Brampton, Ontario
L6S 6A7 Canada

www.wtlipublishing.com

ISBN 978-0-981075-91-4

Printed in the USA

10 9 8 7 6 5 4 3 2 1

TABLE OF CONTENTS

TEARS FOR ANOTHER

Carson just wanted to fit in. Sitting in a dimly lit room amongst shady characters, he felt unsettled but tried to appear cool. Surprisingly invited to "party" with some guys—guys he thought were cool—he accepted their invitation without hesitation.

Now after an hour and a half of being the butt of their jokes and drinking heavily, he regretted his choice to join them; after all, it was a detour—a distraction. Carson was hitchhiking from a place I cannot remember to Toronto to find his mother who had abandoned him. He wanted to help her and free her from her crack addiction. No phone number, address or even a region within Toronto that was connected to Carson's mother was known yet, and here he was. A sixteen-year-old boy was traveling with no money, searching for the mother that had abandoned him to follow a man and her drug addiction (her boyfriend was one of her addictions and the supplier of her other one); and now he was somewhere very wrong.

The short, burly one among the group started calling Carson a fa@*!t. The others snickered and joined in. They started to suggest how much he would love prison. The laughing became more sinister as they continued to taunt him.

On the streets, your instincts are all you have. You live by them and you die by them. Danger was present and the hairs on Carson's forearms were standing erect and visible to the naked eye. The tallest and meanest of the group looked coldly and purposefully in Carson's eyes as he asked him if he enjoyed the feel of a man's manhood in his mouth—silence. The air was heavy. A line had been crossed, and taunting had now birthed something more sinister. The silence in the room was being rivaled by the pounding in Carson's ears, his blood now surging through his veins, his body prepared for action. His heart mimicked the staccato bursts of a rapid fire weapon unloading its cargo, which he knew from the video games he played.

The sudden sound of the wooden chair screeching against the hardwood floor that was made as the tall one stood up was

3

terrifying. Carson was already standing up and the rest were soon on their feet too, advancing with purpose. Beatings and robbery become a part of your life on the street but this was different. Everyone in the room knew what was about to happen. One never knows what they will do when their back is up against the wall. Desperation spawned a plan. A plate showcasing a half-eaten pizza slice sat on a nearby counter. Carson grabbed it. The plate was cold but so were his hands, which were now moist with sweat. The plan was to smash the plate on the floor and startle his would-be rapists, but his hands were clumsy with fear and soaked now as if the pores of his skin were vomiting sweat, retching from fear. The plate slipped inwards. The testosterone fueling the act made the strike powerful. In one swift movement the plate shattered against Carson's hand, deeply slicing open his thumb and cutting a vein. The appendage looked as if it were threatening to sever completely.

Oddly, it wasn't the pain but the reaction in the faces of the other men in the room that alerted Carson to the hot maroon liquid, thin with alcohol, now painting an abstract piece on his pants and the already-stained floor. The others ran and Carson did so as well, as far as his feet could take him. He dared not stop lest he pass out and die of blood loss.

At my desk sits a boy with a cast on his left hand, innocent, frail and in tears. I open my mouth to ask him a question to complete my paperwork. I cannot speak. My words are enslaved with emotion as my personal worries have cowered away, overpowered by this boy's reality. This is the only time I have ever felt to cry for another man's torment, much less a stranger's. I fight back the tears to remain strong for him. Carson informs me that the doctors said he might lose his thumb. He seems to have accepted this possible fate. He looks me directly in the eyes and returns to his only true ambition as he asks me if I think he will find his mother. His eyes widen slightly with youthful hope as his tears begin to fill the corners. I know my eyes mirror Carson's. I cannot find the words or the strength to utter the bitter truth but I know I don't have to. My eyes have betrayed me—the eyes always do.

I never saw Carson again.

A COLD HEART THAWS

When you work in a field where suffering and struggle are ever apparent, you eventually become less sensitive to it. It is as if your body and soul create a defense against infection. Hopelessness, despair and depression are as contagious as love, hope and compassion. Never convince yourself otherwise.

As a youth worker, you begin to see patterns in people's stories and experiences, and although an awful circumstance may be new and traumatic to a young person, it is the average day for you. I believe the better you are at helping others, the more you begin, at first, to see your clients' situations as problems to be solved, but this is where the warm heart begins to frost. When you "know" you can help and *fix* someone's current problems, frustration may set in if the person is not ready to be *fixed*. True change must happen at the pace of the person or people who are changing, not those that desire that change for them. This is the biggest and probably the most painful part of serving those who are struggling. In the field of social work we are there to be empathetic, to support, to guide and, where possible, to protect. Fixing is not part of the equation.

Sam was a heavy-set boy. He suffered from depression and was slightly delayed in his cognitive abilities. Suffering from an apparent mental disorder that was yet to be diagnosed, he could be difficult to work with at times. Sam constantly threatened to urinate on breakfast, to burn the place down, and to kill himself. He was crying out for attention and help.

Staff attempted to help Sam by setting him up with counsellors, specialists and other support workers. They even arranged an eye test for him to receive free glasses, but this was to no avail. He had a defeated attitude and soon he defeated me. Dealing with a person suffering from depression is no easy task. It is a daily war to combat the depression in the person suffering and to not let it defeat your drive to make supportive efforts. The issue here is that you cannot defeat depression in another person. You can simply support one's overcoming and management of it within themselves. I did not fully understand this at the time.

It was a long overnight shift. My eyes were extremely bloodshot as they often get when sleep is scarce. At the time, this particular shelter operated in the afternoons and evenings, and closed early in the mornings. Part of my job was to wake the youth up, feed them and get them ready to exit the building and begin their day. I joked with the kids, as we usually did, about my red eyes and how I looked like I had just smoked a pound of marijuana with a particular rapper who was infamous for the habit. Sam came downstairs and, to tease me, asked me if he should pee on the sandwiches or the scrambled eggs. I suggested both—why leave anything to chance? He stuck his tongue out and said, "I'm leaving here today. F@!k this world" (he said this every morning). We followed what had become routine: the protocol. Sam knew what to say and a hospital trip was averted. A few kids yelled at him to shut up while others said, "Go ahead!"

It was a smooth morning. Everything went well and we closed up on time. That night I arrived for my shift and was informed that Sam had taken his life by jumping in front of a train. There is no way to have known Sam's plans or if that morning he had indeed intended to have his last day unfold the way it had.

Sam was a very sarcastic person. He was also very gentle in nature. I enjoyed our daily quips and his sharp sense of humour and I know that he enjoyed mine. What I grappled with upon learning of his demise was my own routineness and coldness. That night, as I sat at home nursing Wray & Nephew, watching the ice cubes shrink and dance in an intoxicating manner, I felt something I hadn't felt in a while; it was that familiar heavy lump in the throat you get when your heart weighs heavy. The left side of my face became slightly wet and warm as I sipped from my drink and smiled. I have Sam to thank for reminding me that to appreciate the full picture, you must feel each stroke the brush has made.

THE LAMB
THAT KILLED A
WOLF

Trevor was over-bearing in a charming way. He was loud, abrasive and known amongst clients and staff to tell elaborate tails of street cred and "banging broads" in the trap. Trevor was a gangster wannabe. He used the N word incessantly. Only the F word was used more frequently.

Once you get old enough you get to see the norms and customs you came up with change and disappear. In my high-school days, a guy like Trevor was the type of kid that would get beat up daily. Now his type had become the norm. The loud and "too hard" are feared now. Before they would be written off as fake because no one living the life they claimed would be so obvious. Trevor and the kids like him wore their emotions on their sleeves. In that way they were more transparent than the hardest people I knew growing up; if they loved you they would tell you and hug you every time they saw you.

I liked Trevor but I dislike being lied to and Trevor was king of lies, a liar who lied without fear of being seen as a liar. He had behavioral issues that may have run deeper than I knew but he liked me and always made a big to do when I arrived: 'This my n!@@a! I love this guy! You know how far back me and my dude go? Y'all don't know this muthaf@#ka like I know him. He's been knowing me from time, yo.'

One day I came in and got a big reception. I love the kids and they love me. I let them know so they let me know too when we see each other. This day, I was just as loud as the youth. We were happy to see each other, pounds and hugs all around. Trevor walked up with an exaggerated hood walk, looked right, then left, and leaned in. "I gotta talk to you my n!@@a," he said, barely audible. Resisting the impulse to roll my eyes, I told him to let me get settled as I just got in. He replied, "Nah, n!@@a. Now!" Trevor was upset and his eyes were pleading for an immediate audience. I took him upstairs to my office, closed the door for privacy and asked him, "What's up?" He told me, I was a "lion among snakes," and that he had overheard my coworkers speaking ill of me: "They don't like you, fam. I couldn't wait until I saw you to let you know." It turned out he was telling the truth, a truth I learned a few days later. He told me he had to go to a place to lay low because the "feds" were looking for him. I almost laughed out loud. He asked me for a token. I signed one out for him, gave him daps and a hug and bid him farewell. He jogged out of the building as if they were coming any second, his pants almost around his knees. The sight made me laugh out loud as I remembered his jail stories and his well-rehearsed story of the person he murdered that he used to tell.

Moments later we had a shift change. I told the staff what had just transpired and was interrupted by a coworker, "I know Trevor talks mad s*!t but you know he did kill someone as a kid in jail, right?" I could not believe my ears; of all of his exaggerations and lies, I would not have guessed the most serious and least mentioned story was true. As we looked through the office window, police approached my coworker at the front desk. My coworker called the extension to the phone in the office where we were and said that the police were there to question Trevor.

It was later that Trevor said they "tried him in the showers" and he "ain't 'bout that f*$$#t s*!t. "Bop bop! [Making a stabbing motion] Take that! I handled that," and apparently he did. I had a new understanding of him, not because he murdered someone but because when his back was against the wall, he fought. He fought for his life and that, I can relate to. Context is everything.

I used to speak to Trevor about his poor treatment of some of the mentally ill and other guys in the shelter. He was a nice guy and I wanted him to extend his compassion to them. In the years that I have worked, I have encountered several youth that have been to jail and have been sexually assaulted and others who suffered in silence at the hands of family members. The youth who suffered these sexual atrocities were often left confused about their sexual orientation. I knew of a few youth who maintained poor hygiene as a defense mechanism, others whose mental state and sense of self were forever shattered. Please believe me when I tell you, the only thing I have personally seen break the human spirit more than the loss of a loved one or the deepest depths of addiction is rape. I believe Trevor knew this and every time he saw certain youth, it reminded him of how close he came to drowning in an unexplainable abyss that I believe he feared he would not have come back from.

GUCCI THIS, PRADA THAT

Every so often you will get a diva (male or female) that has fallen on hard times. There is a general misconception that all homeless people are poor. There are certain circumstances that may bring a person from wealth into a homeless shelter. For many, their connection to wealth is like that of a mortgagee to a property; they don't truly own the capital with which they align themselves. In this instance, the mortgagee was a pretty, South Asian woman with her head held high and her dark Chanel glasses that obstructed the view of her perfectly done eyebrows. She demanded to speak to the manager and no one else. When asked to wait she refused to sit in the chair offered to her.

The dinner she was served was waived away upon arrival and a brief inspection; Pria was a snob. I understood her well because, to be honest, I was one too when I first started my career. The difference between Pria and me was that I chose to enter the system; she did not.

It would have been extremely easy to take personal offence to Pria's behavior because she often referred to her life of wealth and when speaking casually, elevated her culture as superior to others'. As expected, this behavior went on for approximately a week or so.

When Pria came through the doors for the first time she was the vision of confidence. Her nose was held high in the air. Brand names were apparent on every piece of her outfit, obnoxiously so, like that of someone trying to show their wealth as opposed to their fashion sense. Her walk was exaggerated yet somehow perfect, as if rehearsed.

The façade was convincing but, truth be told, Pria was scared and was putting on her bravest face. The air of superiority she created around herself was her defense bubble: "Don't mess with me. I'm an important person," it spoke.

It is amazing how quickly the things we use to define us fall away when they no longer serve a purpose or have relevance. Pria came from a world where socio-economic status meant something and appearing wealthy was a must.

In an environment where wealth is not readily attainable, status is not derived from how you look but rather what value you can offer others. In this new world of shelter life, Pria was worse than poor. Her network was non-existent and the people who were not staff that had influence did not speak the same social language she did. Pria soon relaxed her judgment and would sit in the same room as other clients but was generally disengaged. Some of the youth would casually poke fun as a way to joke with Pria and address her snobbery, and she would graciously accept her role. Pria was smart deep down, smarter than her attitude allowed her to be on the surface. I sensed this was not the first time she was subdued by her social position.

One night, a dinner of frozen, pre-cooked chicken fingers, instant soup, salad and frozen vegetables was served. Pria protested and while speaking to a staff member who was sitting with her, stated that when she lived in Vancouver she loved eating fresh seafood and scallops, not this "crap." Her comments were heard by another resident who had had enough of her high society poise. He quickly snapped at her and yelled, "Stupid b!#*h! Why don't you go back to your mansion if you're so rich? Go *** [expletives] and get your rent paid or shut up!" The verbal altercation that ensued was interrupted by staff. Both youth were removed from the dining area and taken to separate offices to process. Pria ended up in the main office with me. She was furious. She demanded that the other youth be discharged (now called a service restriction). She asked how we could let him speak to her, or any woman, like that— I let her vent and get it out. What the other resident had done was speak to the elephant in the room. He, in effect, asked the logical question that begged to be answered, "If you come from a better life, why are you here?" Pria had not opened up to any staff yet and now was not the time to speak to that issue.

I thanked Pria for not escalating the situation further, for being open-minded about the conditions she now found herself in (she hadn't been) and for conducting herself with class and self-respect. I was handling her and she knew it but I was speaking a language she couldn't refuse. This incident was beneath her and she had to drop it once it was openly challenging her civility. Now we could have a conversation. I admitted to Pria that I too don't find pre-cooked and processed foods appetizing and informed her that in my culture we don't eat these things much either. Looking her in the eye, I said, "…but when in Rome, you do as the Romans do." I let her eyes follow mine as I looked into the dining room. Pria asked, "Is that why you eat the food also? Not all staff eat with them. Are you hungry? Do you not eat at home?" I laughed and she smiled coyly. On the surface we were speaking casually but here, Pria was testing me—testing my patience, my temperament, my status and how safe she was with me. I told Pria my Costco card was put to good use. She laughed and nodded. I then challenged her to consider how it might feel to someone who grew up in a poor family that could only afford these types of meals to constantly hear her chastise their upbringing. Pria was sharp and understood immediately. I continued and explained that I eat the food and sit in the common areas so that the youth and I can build rapport and trust each other when we need to discuss sensitive issues. Pria sensed that I was speaking about her. Having planted that seed I changed direction. I finished by challenging Pria to find a way to let her guard down and to connect with some of the other youth while remaining true to herself. She promised she would.

Later that evening while playing cards, I suggested to the youth that I was playing with to switch to a game of dominoes. They enthusiastically accepted my offer. Dominoes is a game that is popular locally amongst many descended from the Caribbean. Many who play usually get loud and boisterous, brag and size up each other. It's played like a game of chess, Caribbean style. You can play dominoes quietly but that would be as fun as playing a close game of charades in hush tones. Dominos was a game enjoyed by many of the cool, loud and confident residents who identified with urban culture at some level. This was not a game Pria would naturally play, so I invited her to play. She nervously walked over and said, "Nathan, you know I don't know how to play!" I pulled up a chair beside me and said, "That's why I'm going to teach you, silly." She nervously smiled. Delroy, who was sitting at the table to play, started washing the dominoes (the term used for shuffling or mixing them up before players drew their hands) and said to Pria, "Come, my gyal. Learn de ting and get your first six love from a boss." [Come, my girl. Learn the game and get your first 6 love from a master.] Another player countered stating, "Nah fam, a mi dat! She a ga fall fi de don." [No comrade, that's me (not you)! She is going to fall to the true master right here!] This talk confused Pria not only because of the seemingly sexual nature of it but because she had heard these guys speak proper English before. The game of dominoes often brought out the native

27

tongue of the parents of the youth who played it (or the best rendition of it they could achieve). The third player was a girl named Jessi. She was chatty and loved Jamaican culture but was not native to the community. Jessi, happy to be the advising expert for Pria, patted her on the hand and said, "Don't worry, hun. 'Love' in dominoes is when you lose to the winner six times." We played and on our second hand I had hard end on both sides. No one else could play accept for us, which in this case is called having "key." Pria, seeing it was our turn and seeing the domino, knew we had won. I told her to stand up and slam it on the table and say something celebratory. She stood up. Delroy threw his hands up in the air in feigned protest as she slammed the domino down and yelled, "Boom! Boom!" Jessi said, "I think you mean, 'Bam! Bam!'" We all laughed. Pria had been accepted and had more games to play. I excused myself to go work in my office and from there, I could still hear the raucous laughter and playful shouting from the game.

Pria came to the shelter with $700.00 to her name, practically broke in her eyes. She knew how to spend money but not how to make it. A recent divorcee of an abusive husband, she had made it to Toronto from Vancouver and was on the run.

Pria had been imprisoned by a life that had her in a role as an aging arm piece to be seen and not heard, lavished by a man who held over her an account of all of the gifts he bought her. She would later tell us, she was lucky the rare times she was able to win his affection. When the abuse turned from just physical to humiliation, Pria subconsciously began planning her exit plan by dreaming of leaving.

Once you have learned the life lesson, life tests you on that very lesson. On a sunny day, under a tree in the front of the shelter sat Pria fully engaged in a book she was reading. Nearby, two young emo guys were smoking what they claimed was kush. "The most potent weed on the block," they boasted, while a self-proclaimed Rastafarian youth sat shaking his head in silent protest. He sat on a giant, decorative rock while practicing the formation of a circle with the weed smoke he was exhaling. Seeing staff approaching their smoking area, the guys quickly relocated leaving a thick, pungent cloud of heavy smoke. It was amidst this scene that a newer model Mercedes entered the parking lot, peaking the interest of the other youth relaxing on the grass. A well-dressed man stepped out of the vehicle with disgust as he gave the scene a disapproving once-over. Noticing Pria, he opened the passenger door and glared at her. As if she could feel his presence, she looked up and shock and fear consumed her. I could only imagine what Pria thought. Impatient with her hesitation, he spoke to her authoritatively in another language.

A fellow staff member and I began to intervene and inform the trespasser he needed to leave. The kids now rose to their feet with their attention fixated on this intruder. The situation had just escalated in a matter of two seconds and this had not gone unnoticed by the aggressor that now stopped his advance, visibly intimidated. Pria walked to him calmly. It was obvious she had returned before. He smiled a smile of victory. The slap reverberated throughout the parking lot. All were in shock. Holding his face, the intruder stared at Pria for a second and she stared back at him. Their silence was broken by the other youth that were pointing and laughing. She struck him hard again. He looked as if he were going to cry and then Pria pounced on him, viciously slapping, punching, biting and kicking him. Grunting as we scraped her off him, he retreated to his car and reversed hurriedly to the other end of the parking lot and then sped off. Pria was in tears. She later told me she didn't know why she was crying.

I thanked Pria often after that day for doing what so few did. The number of abused people that make excuses for their abusers and assist in their own captivity, although understandable, is incalculable. Pria reminded me that some do overcome, making it easier and more realistic for me to suggest that others break the cycle and do the same.

POSSESSION IS REAL

It was late and my colleague Roger and I were nearing the end of our shifts. A troubled young lady entered the program inebriated and was regressing quickly as her high was amplified by her mental illness or vice versa. She was a lot heavier than when I saw her months ago, likely made plump by the medication prescribed to her. Becky was a fan of ecstasy and the rave culture that supports it. Most street youth who abuse drugs do so with the passion of a lover, intoxicated with the first fleeting weeks of romance. Desperate for their addiction's next embrace, they lust for every seductive kiss and indulge in panic due to a fading high.

In the midst of briefing for the next shift, Becky started banging on the office door, accompanied by another youth. Roger, my colleague, opened the door to allow Becky to enter. She collapsed on the couch, breathing heavily, panting the way one would if they were to impersonate a dog. We asked Becky what she had taken. She informed us that she had swallowed *twelve* ecstasy pills.

Her communication was sporadic as she began to fade in and out of consciousness. The ebb and flow of an intensifying, unimaginable high was becoming apparent. The paramedics were called and the individual who brought Becky to the office returned to her room. Now on the couch sat a girl who seemed to be deflating before our eyes, her breathing becoming more erratic as she inhaled short, more rapid, consecutive breaths. Holding her chest, her face began to contort as her mouth opened. She was slowly slipping off of the couch. Roger and I rushed to her aid as our instincts took over. Each of us, with an arm under hers, began to hoist her back up as she moaned and turned to me. What happened next, I may never forget. Looking me right in the eyes without blinking, Becky screamed, "Nathan, f@# me! F@#k me! F@#k me!" and continued to repeat the phrase as if it were a chant.

In the social work field, especially when dealing with youth, the threat of being accused of sexual inappropriateness is always present. Now engulfed in what appeared to be a full orgasm, repeating the phrase louder and with more intensity, she began to thrust her body forward. I released my grip. I was new to the field at the time and this was a particularly difficult situation. The many stories of several youth workers accused of sexual irresponsibility that were told to new staff flooded my memory. I was in shock. I was scared. Roger slightly buckled under the weight of a woman losing herself to bodily convulsions. I called the paramedics again to report her worsening condition and awaited instruction. Meanwhile, a female staff member who was on another floor of the shelter had now joined us and was assisting Roger in supporting the erratic, convulsing youth.

Uttering incomprehensible words and thrashing less now than before, Becky was regressing into the deflated state she first assumed when on the couch. Looking visibly exhausted as if her limbs were burdened with cement weights, Becky began to calm down and eventually she passed out. I needed a break. I cannot remember why the paramedics did not arrive but Becky was escorted to her room, a regular occurrence in the low income area surrounding the shelter. The mattress was removed from the bunk bed she had been assigned to and placed on the floor so that she could sleep safely on it.

I would see Becky for several months after that (I had known her through my work at the shelter for a couple of years prior to that day). She would fluctuate in weight from obese to rail thin. The effects of the illegal drugs Becky abused and the prescribed drugs used to combat the damage caused by her addiction and mental illness were taking their toll on her body. Before my eyes I saw this young, bright girl deteriorate into a shell of her former physical and psychological self.

The inner demons that addicts face are real. We are all wired differently. Different things energize and motivate us, but when the hold of addiction drags you deep into the darkest of places it takes all of your spiritual strength to come back.

My stomach turned the last time I saw Becky. She looked deformed from the self-mutilation and neglect she tortured her body with. I felt so much grief for her. Few teeth left, a hole in her cheek large enough to put a small finger through, and hair almost thinned to baldness, I couldn't help but think Becky had already died; her body simply didn't know it yet. I stopped seeing Becky, as she aged out of the youth shelter programs. I hope and pray she didn't succumb to her demons.

SWEET
DREAMS

As an avid fan of music, certain lyrics speak to me rather profoundly upon hearing them. One of those lyrics came from The Eurythmics in their pop hit "Sweat Dreams." The words that spoke to me and millions is the part that says: "Everybody's looking for something. Some of them want to use you. Some of them want to get used by you. Some of them want to abuse you. Some of them want to be abused." All things that live seem to have a recipe or set group of requirements that when present enables them to grow healthy and fruitfully multiply. When certain healthy elements aren't present like two loving parents, safe shelter from the elements, a structured and supportive community, etc., it is easier for suffering to gain a foothold. In my career, one of the hardest things to see is two people caught up in a toxic relationship. When you understand the cyclical psychological and sociological roots of the drama playing out before you, it is even more tragic to witness.

A shelter is ripe with people who are missing necessary elements from a healthy childhood. Young men and women raised seeing, hearing or suffering physical, sexual and verbal abuse carry those experiences into their own relationships and often find discomfort in healthy relationships as they feel foreign and unreal. This cycle is hard to break and takes a substantial amount of effort to overcome it successfully: most importantly it requires the individual's readiness to change, proven through actions (not words), accompanied by a genuine request for help.

Before the rainbow and the peaceful aftermath, must come the storm—corny, I know, but true. There are countless examples I could choose from my career, but Sheila sticks out the most to me. Small and unassuming, Sheila's petite size often gave her the façade of a [traditionally] feminine demeanor: dainty and fragile. Her past, she held closely behind often silent lips. I imagined she was the runt of her siblings. We were not supposed to have favourites but she was a favourite of mine. She took to me too and often shared with me about her thoughts and happenings before she did so with other staff. Sheila was attractive in a natural way. She didn't spend much time or energy on her appearance or on attracting guys although she did attract them.

When she first arrived, being new alone would have been enough to get her initial attention, but her quiet way came off as alluring and her foreign accent made her even more of a commodity. It became quickly apparent that Sheila was cunning and could be manipulative; she would accept gifts of weed, liquor and stolen goods from the boys. She already knew how to give subtle looks and to use her laugh to endear but what made Sheila special and made her a favourite of mine is a guilty confession of mine. Sheila had many subtle weapons but soon it would become apparent that Sheila was hardened by the streets, a bully who would come to fight and intimidate both the boys and girls. She mastered being respected by the right people and never hesitated to throw her knuckles at the face of often taller and larger opponents. One day while she sat in my office and I asked her why she had kicked another youth in the genitals, slapped him in the face and spat on him her reply was simple: "I told him that if he didn't get out of my seat, I would slap the s#!t out of him and he laughed, so I gave it to him." Sheila spoke plain as day as if she were reading the newspaper out loud. I pointed out to her that she did more than slap him. There was that sly grin I came to know well and she coyly said, "He was too tall, I had bring him down first to reach his face." She laughed and internally smiling, I shook my head and read her the riot act.

On another stay at that shelter I was pleased to see she had returned and was safe. Looking at her for the first time in a while, I noticed she was coming into her own womanhood. Her long curls were now let down and the clothes were less baggy and masculine. What intrigued me about Sheila wasn't her ruthlessness but the duality of her nature even though I hadn't yet understood the randomness of it. She could be fighting on behalf of someone being bullied and the next moment she was the bully threatening a beating while emptying a victim's pockets. More than Sheila's appearance had changed. The role she played within the shelter had also changed.

I had learned that the nearby gang that she was thought to be a part of had now become upset with her, meaning her physical safety was constantly at risk. You see, Sheila wasn't super-human; her power had realistic source. She did have strength beyond what would generally be assumed of someone her size, coupled with a willingness to fight cruelly and viciously, but she was also backed.

44

Many of the guys she terrorized didn't dare strike her back for fear of her calling her alleged gang-affiliated friends. The nearby gang serviced our youth as well but their service came by way of loans of drugs and money, and protection to privileged people. Having no shortage of impressionable girls, sex alone could not have earned the protection she had; Sheila was one of their drug dealers. Now this connection had been severed, causing her protection to be revoked and her punishment was arranged to be administered on sight. Despite this, Sheila was outside at times. A missing piece was not yet revealed.

Later in my shift a tall, young man entered the shelter to a hero's welcome. He went by the name of Tech and had a reputation the bullies in the shelter respected; when he laughed everyone laughed and when he was upset everyone was quiet. Tech was the alpha male, the one in charge—right under the staff in the power hierarchy. He was the one that protected and disciplined others in the rooms, washrooms, corners and halls that staff couldn't always monitor. Desired by almost all of the women and respected by all the men, Tech would naturally appeal to Sheila, but now even more so as protection was urgently needed. Sheila, being a girl who had not slept with any of the guys in the house (to anyone's knowledge), was a prize herself; naturally she and Tech were a rumoured couple.

Dinner was soon served and Tech was the first to eat. Sheila was second. He got his plate and hers. Anything she wanted, he would get for her: his gesture both an act of chivalry and control. As valuable as his protection might have been, I could see it was also stifling for Sheila. She was always second to him. He was always the personality in the room, while she was always measured and muted in his presence. For most, this would be tough but for Sheila it must have been excruciating. She was unique in that she was naturally a female "boss" and there were only a few that we as staff had seen over the years.

All relationships have a honeymoon period were patience is in abundance, powered by the euphoria of the newness of it all. As the gloss dims and the relationship becomes more real, structure and roles must be set and what the relationship really is starts becoming more apparent.

Sheila started wearing makeup, but the bruised eye she sported one Tuesday evening would have required a movie-set-worthy makeup job to hide. When I saw her, I called out to her to come into my office. She ignored me. I gave Sheila her space. I knew that she knew why I was calling her. Later in the shift, she entered my office, closed the door and hugged me. I opened my mouth to speak but I felt her sobbing. After a few moments, she smiled, composed herself and in her European-soaked accent, she said we'd talk later. And so was the beginning of the descending spiral that would be Sheila and Tech.

Tech, was a psychological terrorist to Sheila. She couldn't do anything right. She was either being asked to dress sexy because he liked that (something she resented because she was still a Tomboy at heart and did not want to dress sexy for a man's contentment), or she was being yelled at for being too sexy and blamed for guys wanting to be with her and for being too flirty. Sheila began to retreat into herself, finding it safer and easier to be quiet and do as little as possible than to risk angering her boyfriend.

At the time, there was another couple that had a relationship that mirrored Tech and Sheila's. Sheila made the mistake of saying something about her relationship to the one who was the controlling partner in the relationship. This person eventually relayed Sheila's complaints to Tech. Tech was furious and beat Sheila so savagely that when the police arrived, he offered himself up. This was after Sheila refused to do so. Face swollen, she sat in the stairwell crying for her boyfriend who had been arrested. Tech already had a prior warrant out for his arrest. Sheila was the talk of the house that evening until the other couple entered my office.

They were a talkative couple with a sarcastic sense of humour. The "Sheila" in this relationship said in a flippant way, "That's why I started dating girls. Guys are a$$*^@#s". The comment offended her girlfriend (I assume she took it as appearing weaker than Tech was) who slapped her hard across the face, grabbed her by the jaw and kissed her. Although they protested and said it was a joke, both of them had to leave that evening and were found beds at other shelters—one, for the abuse, and the other, for their safety. They both called me several names in protest and accused me of being jealous of their "strong" and "real" relationship.

Often people in toxic relationships seem to be lost to the fact that their unions are only "dream partnerships." They are lost as to the nightmarish effect on themselves and the effect their drama has on all who see it. They make excuses and tell loosely constructed lies to explain what we are seeing. Sometimes sweet dreams are made of this: the need to escape a nightmarish reality.

INVESTING IN MONSTERS

...And then there is the thug, not the bully, not the affiliated or surface gang member, but the seasoned criminal. This type of youth has been in and out of jail and has committed some crimes that are more serious than misdemeanors. Violence is not only accepted but embraced by this person as a tool and as a form of communication. Normally, such a person would only be found in a shelter for one or a combination of four reasons: one, they are not good at crime and therefore are not successful at getting away with or making a profit at it; two, they are fresh out of jail and are court-ordered to stay at the shelter; three, they genuinely like their life at the shelter as opposed to their life outside of it; or four, they have somewhere to stay but remain in the shelter to engage in illegal activity, e.g., pimping or selling stolen goods, drugs or cigarettes.

When you watch the news or read someone's file it is easy to see them through that lens solely. When you hear about a youth who, for instance, beat an elderly lady nearly to death to rob her of pocket change, it is hard to think that they may be charming, kind or shy. I remember as a kid watching TV documentaries or the news, whenever they would interview someone who knew the accused, the description of the accused usually wasn't of a hardened criminal. Although one cannot use such descriptions to justify criminal actions, the understanding that crimes are actions and not character definitions of people can drastically broaden one's understanding of the world around them.

I have known child molesters, rapists, murderers, drug dealers, abusive parents, abusive children, abusive boyfriends, abusive girlfriends, and so on. For several years, I worked in two very different youth shelters and often I would encounter a youth who would frequent or even register at both. (This was very common prior to the city implementing an online, real-time registry).

I remembered the first time I met Sam. Tiny and sickly looking, Sam had an awkward sense of humour coupled with awkward social skills; Sam was a "nerd". He loved to tell jokes that weren't funny to others and had no reservations about laughing out loud at them. Admirably, he was the type of resident that was generally always in a good mood. Like many shelter youth (especially males), Sam gave himself an alias, "Whites" (for his extremely pale skin), and would re-tell his story of armed robbery and jail time to anyone who would listen. Whites was not a thug but desperately tried to impress them and, oddly enough, saw himself as one of them. Often Whites would be given a pass by others, seen as someone too weak to earn any stripes from punking him and too innocent and nerdy to recruit—he was safe.

There had not been any significant event that had occurred in my presence with Sam that I could remember. Shortly after meeting him, I went over the notes in his file to help prepare a plan of action for his case management. Amongst his notes were limited references to the molestation of an infant sibling. I was disgusted and angry once I discovered his secret. Children are so innocent. They reflect the best, yet most vulnerable side of us. Naturally they are a difficult area for me to remain non-judgmental about. Sam was the monster in the basement, a member of the most degenerate amongst us. I would often shake my head when he presented his story of robbery as being the reason why he had been in jail. And still, Sam needed to eat, needed a plan to get him out of the system and reintegrated into society, needed winter clothes, needed structure and most of all, needed acceptance. In dealing with Sam, I willfully forgot what he had done in his past so I could properly serve him with the support he needed.

Whites, as he increasingly began to insist on being called, had an awkwardness that amused another resident in the program. This resident was the exact opposite of Whites.

Built like a tank and prone to violence, he was what the other youth pretended to be. Mason had done lots of time. He literally was in and out of jail. He was quiet as well but not in a sheepish way. He used his silence to intimidate and his screwface (Toronto slang for a scowl) to menace.

Something about Whites spoke to Mason and Whites became his jester, always telling jokes and seeking his approval. This was one of the more ironic occurrences we often saw play out beyond our office windows. You see, Mason had been neglected and sexually abused by an uncle in his youth. He harboured a lot of pain and likely would have killed Whites had he known of Whites' secret. Adversely, Whites was neglected at a young age in the sad, yet all-too-familiar scenario of a single mother who chose her boyfriend over her child. Although the act was inexcusable to me, this was this situation that led Sam to sodomize his infant sibling.

Sam's mother was never much of a parent, according to Sam's version of events told to a counsellor (prior to my meeting him). She fed and clothed him but he was more of a burden than blessing, a glaring reminder of a life of bad decisions. When Sam's mother met someone new and had a child with that person, it was a new beginning for her. The pregnancy was a happy one and not a mistake. The unborn baby had a room filled with gifts awaiting its arrival, a room that was once Sam's. Not being a rich family, a larger place wasn't an option, Sam's new room became the living room where he slept on a sofa bed. Sam's mother did suggest to her boyfriend that they get a larger apartment to accommodate her son but she was stonewalled. The new boyfriend was not a fan of Sam, the son of another man living under the roof he helped pay for. The boyfriend informed the mother that she need not worry about Sam's sleeping on the couch because he had a year to find a job and pay half of the rent or get out. Sam's mother had tried to make it on her own and wasn't going to jeopardize losing a man with a job. Sam got the message and finally saw himself through his mother's eyes (he believed) for the first time: Sam's birth was a burden to his mother while the new pregnancy was a blessing. Months of perceived rejection and inner hate built up and boiled over into one unforgiveable act of vengeance that would fulfill the impression he believed his mother had of him.

Sam once told me I was one of his favourite staff members. He thought I was cool and funny, "mad jokes," as he put it. I heard that Sam moved on with no further issues. I have often been asked how I can stand dealing with some of the people we serve that have committed the most offensive acts. When I answer, I often think of youth like Sam. In truth, the longer you deal with someone, the more removed from their past they will be in your mind (if their past and present actions are polar opposites). On a more conscious level though, a seasoned social worker is well aware of cycles: cycles of poverty, cycles of abuse and cycles of pain (among others). Many have heard the age-old wisdom that if you treat someone like a criminal, they will become one. Well, it is also true to say that they will remain one. You reap growth were you invest; if you invest and focus on the negative actions or aspects of a person, then that is what is nurtured. Positivity and negativity are both like kinds of weeds within us. The kind that is allowed to grow is the kind that will bear fruit. If I tell you daily that you are smart and I treat you like you are intelligent, you will eventually act smarter and invest in gathering knowledge, further feeding your intelligence. With the Sams out there, I am so offended by what they have done and the thought of them amongst society hurting people, that I double down. I can't change laws. Hurt people hurt people. All any of us can do is help the healing process.

FOCUS

Sometimes the most important lessons about work ethic and achievement come from people immersed in misfortune. In this regard, shelter life is an academy of sorts.

I barely saw the European duo, a pair of brothers known for their work ethic. They kept to themselves and rarely engaged with other youth. One looked like a slight variation of the other, often making it hard to discern one from the other. I admired the respect they showed to the staff and their ability to maintain a life outside the shelter bubble. I didn't encounter them much because I worked

61

nights and they worked long hours in construction and slept shortly after they arrived.

The young pair informed a colleague that they planned to leave the shelter soon and had asked for help in finding suitable housing that would meet their budget of $950.00 per month between the two of them. The housing worker asked the brothers to provide a bank statement because he wanted to ensure they had the necessary first and last down payment. It was shared during my shift change (a briefing that occurs between shifts to share pertinent information amongst staff) that the brothers might turn in a statement with their individual balances and if they did, it should be forwarded to the housing worker.

Toward the end of my shift, hungry and heavily soiled in dirt and white paint, the boys entered. Ever humble and respectful, these seemingly simple guys politely asked for dinner and showed no frustration when they were told they had to wait for a few minutes. Just as I was about to leave my office to serve them, I was interrupted by the phone and its incessant ringing. I picked it up and on the other end was a bill collector seeking to harass and shame one of my colleagues at their place of work. A bit surprised by the time they were calling and not in the mood to deal with this abuse of personal information, I hung up and moved toward my office door. Just as I was approaching the door, it opened slowly and the shorter of the two brothers, Milan, produced two small papers from his dirty jean pocket. The boy attempted and failed to pronounce the word "receipts" and we both laughed as I said it properly and assured him he would soon be speaking English better than all of us.

I went downstairs and prepared dinner for the two brothers in a room we used for feeding youth after dinner hours. My shift had been busy. Hours of dealing with fifty-six youth with varying developmental abilities and challenges was beginning to take a toll on my mood and I was exhausted and literally in pain from the growing headache gaining ground beyond my temples. This was my third shift in a row, my twenty-sixth hour of back-to-back work between two jobs, and the ever-constant buzz of a small army of youth was growing to an onslaught best described as a ghetto orchestra reaching its climax. I was almost defeated.

Half way through the door, my daily escape from my employer would have been successful, but I remembered the two small papers from the brothers. I took them from my jacket pocket, unfolded them and studied them. My initial gasp was the first of four as I scanned the small balance sheets and let the numbers, $40,000.00 and $38,000.00 make sense in my mind. My mind shut out the offense of noise from the small army but I was in too much shock to enjoy the first moment of silence I was experiencing during that entire shift. I passed the statements to the staff beginning their shift. Without a word, I turned and opened the door to leave only to find myself five feet from the brothers. Aleksi, the taller brother, looked at me and then looked past me to the other staff in the office. Ironically, the staff member who was being stalked by the bill collector was now holding the financial statements. His look of surprise masked the shame each of us bore inside. If these foreign, homeless youth could amass this small king's ransom in savings in two years, each of us should have been millionaires. Aleksi, now dawning an awkward smile, in poor English stammered, "We save good?"—"Yes, Aleksi, you save good."

THE WEALTH OF THE "FIRST WORLD'S" POOR

Short, innocent, humble and cheerful: these were the words that came to mind when I first met Dac Kien. He was a foreigner in Toronto on a student visa who arrived at our shelter because his student grants had been exhausted during his first semester. Dac Kien was usually happy and willing to do his share in chores, to partake in several of the robust conversations the youth would have and to help anyone who asked him for his aid. A rough, developing, yet fresh, grasp of the English language did not seem to deter him at all. In fact, I think he was more social in an attempt to communicate in English better. In everything that he partook, he was cheerfully fearless and always willing to try something new. What I instantly liked about Dac Kien was that he understood the duty every individual had toward the greater harmony of the larger group, a concept lost to many of his peers at the shelter. An avid student, Dac Kien would come home from school, eat dinner with everyone, do a chore and then retire to a room we reserved for him to study in. His manner of studying was unique but paid homage to the idea that you learn best by teaching. Dac Kien would dictate his lessons out loud to himself, and on occasion, to someone else via a computer. For hours he would study, only ceasing in order to retire to bed.

Dac Kien possessed many redeeming qualities but what touched me the most was displayed the one and only time I remember seeing him angered. Several of the youth became dissatisfied with the food and lack of variety over approximately two weeks. It was explained that much of the food was donated and that the menu was, in large part, restricted by this fact. At times, the youths' expectations and senses of entitlement were extreme—a result of what I would imagine is a need to exert control on one of the only parts of their lives that was safe and structured.

During one of the dinners where protest had grown loud and verbally abusive to the chef, Dac Kien's composure broke. As the cook served that night's meal of rice and chicken stew with both pork and vegetarian options, standing quickly to his feet the way one would if they jumped out of their seat after being startled, Dac Kien spoke and did so forcefully. Gone was the humble, soft-spoken nature he was known for. Rather now stood a young man emboldened by what appeared to be disgust. Loudly, he declared, "All of you are spoiled! Where I am from, this place is a hotel and these daily buffets are for the rich." Visibly emotional, he went on stating how he sometimes felt guilty eating meat and having seconds every night at dinner time when neither was a regular choice for him or his family back home. The most impactful thing he said was the last point he made (one often shared amongst staff of immigrant heritage). Dac Kien went on to inform the youth that the rest of the world was not like Canada. 'When you are poor and homeless in most of the rest of the world, you live on the street; there is no such thing as a shelter or government money to save you—you beg and steal to survive.' I was astounded at the reality check and taken aback by the honesty and raw emotion of his personal testimonial. I was not alone. The room was silent and apologies to the chef were muttered. Dac Kien finished his food as other youth began to echo his sentiments and supported him for sharing. Once finished eating, he cleaned his plate, asked for the room he studied in to be opened and once again became immersed in his studies.

Not all valuable lessons are new ones. I have been thankful for meeting Dac Kien and the reminder he gave us all that day. I was not surprised when I came to find that though he had not even graduated, he was in the media being hailed as one of Canada's top academics. I know he felt lucky to have his experience in Canada but I feel we were just as lucky to have him.

THE N!@@A TREATMENT

Growing up in the '80s, racism in Toronto was very different from what it is today, as the generation before would say of my generation. I clearly remember being the only black male in my school. My fifth grade teacher would dismiss me regularly from class to stand outside (literally! Our class was in a portable) for speaking while she was teaching, regardless of whether I had been speaking or not. This was what she called "going to Siberia." On the last day of school before summer, my teacher gave farewell cards to all of the kids in our class. My card said, "Have a great summer, Nathan. Keep on dancing." I had never danced or even mentioned dancing in that woman's presence. When I grew up in Malton, my family was just starting out like many of the other immigrants in that community. We were white, black, brown and every shade in between; we were human. I didn't know I was black before I lived in Brampton. I knew I was half Ghanaian, half Barbadian, and an African Canadian, but I did not know what racial colours meant. My skin was darker than some of my friends, the same way my hair was stronger than some of theirs, but I was oblivious to these facts.

The first time I heard the N-word was when a classmate of mine was called it. She cried. I knew it was a bad word but it had no effect on me prior to this event. Now it made

74

my Italian friend cry and I began to realize the weight of this word.

Racism is funny in that since it is illogical it is flexible in its use. At the time, Italians and "blacks" were seen similarly and suffered the same caricatures; we both were thought of as sexual masters, overly macho with little intelligence. I knew this even at that age thanks to TV (Remember The Fonz?). I learned at a young age that in Malton, the humility of being at the bottom, or rather, the beginning, did not provide the luxury of racism. Survival was paramount. There wasn't really a large enough population of any ethnic group at the time to practice seclusion (the Italians, Portuguese and Jamaicans were the largest I could remember). I had a white uncle, Tom (yeah, I know), who was a schoolmate of my father's who did magic tricks. My parents rented out our basement to a white couple who went hunting up North and would bring deer meat for us. They also took me to my first hockey game. My best friend was Jamaican and I often watched cartoons at my Irish friend's house. Your neighbours were your support system. They were informal babysitters; they were your other parents, peering from their porches or watching through screen doors over the neighbourhood kids. Sadly, this close knit community is a luxury often lost as you move to a wealthier postal code these days.

Fast forward to present day and now the word I hate is used everywhere. I have heard a male from every culture refer to himself as one. I have heard countless "white" girls with "black" boyfriends or men who are the fathers of their children use the word. All my favourite rap artists except for Eminem and myself used the word as well. Although I hate the casual use of the word, I admire how far those who have been closely tied to it have come and I feel positive about the rest of the journey we must go.

One day, I found myself sitting in my office with a youth named Jason who was retelling his story of being harassed and then beaten by the police before being thrown into jail for the weekend (I hear stories like these all of the time). In my head, I was looking at this white kid, dressed in baggy Hip Hop clothes who had, in the past, told me that he is one eighth Jamaican on his mother's side along with being an eighth First Nations, an eighth Scottish, an eighth British, an eighth Irish, an eighth Spanish, and so on, and I was thinking—*riiiiiight!* I had heard this all of the time too. Just tell me you like the culture and we're good. There's no need to lie. It's funny that I hear the same breakdown from black people who think a little bit of another culture creates this notion of exoticism by mixed heritage and has added value.

Jason's account of how his weekend went was also all too familiar amongst shelter youth. Often it was a story of them doing nothing wrong and the police harassing them. Regardless of colour, being young and marginalized will get you the "n!@@a treatment." Retail stores don't want you there (nor whole malls for that matter), movie theatres don't want you there, schools tolerate you, immature police officers disproportionately harass you, and even others receiving the same treatment are conditioned to trust you only very cautiously. Remember, racism is based on a fallacy. While there is support for the argument that distinct classifications can be made based on phenotypic and genetic characteristics among humans, the human race is one race. There is good evidence that diversity is a continuum rather than a matter of distinct categories of race. There are cultures and creeds but these are ever-changing, and therefore, the idea of race and racism itself can be flexible, adjustable and transferable. As comedian Katt Williams once joked, "We [can] all be n!@@as now." The point is that Jason, as a white, marginalized youth was being treated like what the N-word connoted.

That weekend, a friend's birthday party was being celebrated in what used to be the club district on Richmond Street. I used to throw weekly events at clubs so I was asked to handle the arrangements at a particular club in the heart of Toronto. I negotiated a flat rate amongst my friends that would afford enough bottles for us to have all the drinks we could want for the night. The night went smoothly inside the club. I was handling a lot of money and I was driving that that day so I had only two drinks. I was kind of bored but everyone else seemed to be having fun, so "mission accomplished." We were all outside and Richmond Street was busy with people exiting the cluster of clubs in the area. My friend Greg had work in the morning and needed a taxi to get home. I decided to help him. I had forgotten, though, how hard it was for a black man to get a cab in the city at a decent hour, never mind at 3:00 a.m. on Richmond Street. Car after car slowed down and then sped off as we approached. Even when we got white girls to flag the cabs down, they would speed up once they saw who the passenger would be. My blood was boiling. I instantly knew we were suffering the n!@@a treatment and I wasn't having it! The next car was driven by an East African man with a thick accent. He slowed down and I caught a glimpse of him. I thought, *finally, a brother*. He looked at me and said, "No black guys, sorry." I was stunned, ashamed of him, and livid. I said, "But you are black!" He just repeated himself. I felt the anger take over me and as he drove off slowly, I smacked the back of the cab. My adrenaline was high and the trunk reverberated at the impact. Everyone but the taxi driver froze; he sped off. I stepped into the middle of the street, determined that another taxi would not pass us by without taking Greg. As I stood there, I felt someone swing me around from behind and grab me by my shirt. As a reflex, I too grabbed him by the collar. It was an officer. He was surprised at the force as was I. I wasn't doing anything warranting being touched, surely not without at least being addressed first. Still holding each other, I opened my mouth to ask him what was going on. That was my second mistake. His partner, from behind me, stuffed his forearm deep into my mouth. I thought he would break my jaw. They both took me down. The officer behind me held my hands behind my back. I was on my stomach and the other officer now was punching the back and the side of my head. This all was on a crowded street on Richmond. I don't know if it was the adrenaline but I felt no pain. My eyes were open and what I saw looked like the view from a video camera that was being hit hard. The thought occurred to me that this guy was pummeling my head. I thought I was going to die.

This altercation angered me so much that all I could think was to be calm. I told myself, *you will either pass out or have to defend yourself when he stops*. I heard a friend and fellow promoter call out my name, "Yo, stop! That's "Verse," he said. "He works with kids in the community. What the f@#k are you doing?" Others started to join in: bouncers, club patrons, my friends. That promoter was Celebrity Drew and he probably saved me from brain damage. I could feel the handcuffs, cold and tight. They were used to pull me to my feet. I was furious. I looked the cop in the eyes and said, "You feel good...? Beat a man while he is held on the ground. You punch like a @*$$!"—Not the most tactful or sensible thing to say at that moment but it was how I felt.

A crowd was around us now and people who witnessed were upset. A guy yelled, "I got it all on camera! The face of a female officer was showing concern. She knew something was wrong. They directed me somewhere and I asked where they were taking me. The reality of what had just happened and what I had said sunk in and I thought they were going to beat me all night long. A voice behind me said, "You're going to jail, buddy." I laughed out loud at the absurdity of it all and asked what for. The response: "For public intoxication." I said, "Give me a sobriety test now," and then I was told to shut-up. I was put in the back of a paddy wagon that was like it was made for leprechauns. My knees were against my chest and my body's weight was on the handcuffs that were on my wrists, I sarcastically thought: *my taxes hard at work.*

Me and a large, Russian man sat for what seemed like an eternity. Throughout the night—during the strip search, the endless cop-talk, the eight hours in a holding cell and the constant denial of a phone call or a sobriety test (apparently it's a misconception that you are entitled to either if you are being held for less than twenty-four hours)—all I

84

could think was I am going to fight this. I was released and I walked to my parked car, drove the Russian home and then went to the hospital to have my injuries recorded. I hadn't looked at my face but my cousin who was a nurse was working at the hospital and I could see in her face that my appearance was shocking. I went to my parent's home and my mother tried to downplay her response. I later called my friend Rob and told him what happened and how I planned to fight back and sue. I told him how those cops messed up because I was out with a group of lawyers. He patiently waited and calmly said, "Verse, I'm going to tell you what is going to happen. Are you ready?" I told him to go on and he replied, "Nothing!" I was indignant. I dismissed his truth. I called my lawyer friends and got well wishes but no support. It turned into the run around. I was getting the n!@@a treatment from my friends of all colours in the legal field. No young lawyer wanted to take on the police. Without saying it outright, I felt like everyone was saying, "get over it!"

Jason left the shelter that weekend but he returned again shortly after and he had heard of my ordeal with the police. "I heard they got you too," he said. I responded, "Yeah, but I'm still a pretty playboy!" We both laughed. Looking me in the eyes, he put out his fist to dap me and said, "My n!@@a!" I dapped him and didn't correct him this time. The n!@@a treatment had treated us both as "n!@@as" in that moment. I still hate the word but I now realize the general application of it is sometimes in acknowledgement of the n!@@a treatment. It is flexible and fully applicable to anyone deemed to be worth less than another. I look forward to the abolishment of both the word and the treatment.

www.ingramcontent.com/pod-product-compliance
Lightning Source LLC
Chambersburg PA
CBHW060513280326
41933CB00014B/2955